Scorpio Szn
Copyright © Ella Sadie Guthrie, 2023.

All rights reserved. No part of this book may be used, performed or reproduced in any manner whatsoever without written permission from the publisher except in the case of brief quotations embodied in critical articles or reviews.

First edition.
ISBN 978-1-8380332-9-3

Cover by Casey Ramar
Interior by Angelo Maneage
Edited by Fern Beattie
Proofread by Fern Beattie
Author Photo by Alexander Ward

Typeset in Minion Pro & LFT Etica Mono

Write Bloody UK • London, UK

Support Independent Presses
WWW.WRITEBLOODYUK.CO.UK

SCORPIO SZN

ELLA SADIE GUTHRIE

SCORPIO SZN

CONTENTS

P.	PART ONE
13	FOUND HOROSCOPE FOR A SCORPIO
14	HEARTBREAKER
15	I LIKE THE WAY YOU APPRECIATE THE SINCERITY OF A SHIT MOVIE
16	SPRING
17	READ RECEIPTS ON
19	YOU'RE ON MY MIND
20	TODAY THE SKY IS A SCRATCHCARD
21	SUMMER
22	ELLIPSES
23	CHARLOTTE SAYS NO MORE LOVE POEMS
24	I READ YOUR MESSAGES AGAIN
25	POEM IN RESPONSE TO YOUR PHONE CALL AFTER VALENTINES DAY
26	A SHORT HISTORY OF THE BEDS WE SLEPT IN TOGETHER
27	SAVIOR COMPLEX
28	WHEN WE BROKE UP
29	INFIDELITIES
30	ON SOME SCORPIO SHIT
31	RUTH'S POEM
32	I SAW A TWEET THAT SAID 'MEN BE LIKE "I KNOW A PLACE" AND TAKE YOU TO THE LOWEST POINT IN YOUR LIFE'
33	DREAMING OF MEN
34	SCORPIO SZN
35	SOME MORNINGS I DON'T REMEMBER THAT I LOVE YOU

	PART TWO
39	FOUND HOROSCOPE FOR A LEO RISING
40	PARENT TRAP (1999)
41	AUTUMN
42	I ASK MY MOTHER ABOUT LOVE

43	MEN MAKE ME THIN
44	LEO (RISING)
45	RORY GILMORE DESERVED BETTER
46	WELL SOMEONE HAS TO BE RESPONSIBLE
47	MY FATHER WAS A CROW
48	MIRROR, MIRROR
49	I STOP DRINKING FOR A MONTH
50	I ASK MY FATHER ABOUT LOVE
51	I MEET YOU AT THE MILE STORE
52	MY SISTER AND I DISCUSS YOU BEING NICE TO THE NURSES
53	WHAT IS A TRUTH ANYWAY
54	I WISH I HAD BEEN NICER TO HIM BEFORE I GOT CRAZY
55	THE DRY HEART (1947)
56	FORGIVEN LOVE

PART THREE

59	FOUND HOROSCOPE FOR A PISCES MOON
60	HOW TO WORSHIP
62	JEALOUSY IS MY LOVE LANGUAGE
63	WINTER
64	THE WEST PIER IS STILL BURNING
65	ALL THE MEN ARE CRYING
66	AT ETERNITY'S GATE
68	WE HAD A MOMENT TO REFLECT AND WE CHOSE NOT TO
69	IF WHAT RUMI SAYS
70	CAREFUL OUT THERE, THE WORLD IS BURNING
71	THE WOMAN ALWAYS WEARS HER LOVER'S SHIRT
73	CONSCRIPTION
74	THE SEA WILL KILL YOU IF SHE WANTS TO
75	RING
76	MOON POEM
77	I ASK MY SISTER ABOUT LOVE
78	SIBLING RIVALRY
79	A MOST SATISFACTORY DREAMLIFE
80	I AM WRITING YOU A LOVE POEM ALTHOUGH I KNOW YOU WILL NEVER READ IT
81	SEND MORE LIFE
82	ONLY
83	STAY SOFT
84	SPRING AGAIN
85	FRANK O'HARA NEVER TWEETED

*For everyone I've ever loved
and everyone who's ever had
the misfortune of loving me*

But most of all, for my parents.

PART ONE

*"I used to be very revenge-motivated
but that's just because I'm a Scorpio."*

—SZA

FOUND HOROSCOPE FOR A SCORPIO

THE WORST ███████████████ BUSINESS ██ CAN'T ██
████████████ ACHIEVE ██████████ SUCCESS BECAUSE OF YOUR
████████████ ETHICS. YOU ARE A PERFECT ████████████████
████████ MURDER ███

HEARTBREAKER

We are all just works in progress,
muscles aching and eczema breaking skin.

Our minds playing tricks on us from
old relationships we were in. I confided this

in the pub and you called me a heartbreaker, helped me
eat yellow cheese off cold chips. You ordered

a pint of cider and more chips without cheese. Add salt,
sugar in the form of concentrated tomato. Subtract

the tension, we can't cut it with a plastic knife. *Has
it always been about sex for you?* I think it's always

been a question. When I strolled home that evening,
I wondered what it would take to break a guy like you.

I sent a carrier pigeon to the moon asking if
you'd already been broken, if she was still around

and as I licked vinegar off fingers, cracked open
with raw skin, I wondered what it would take to fix you.

I LIKE THE WAY YOU APPRECIATE THE SINCERITY OF A SHIT MOVIE

and the way you move your shoulders in an awkward dance

when I tell you a joke, pregnant with longing, you smile crookedly
which I thought was an overused literary trope until I saw you do it

baby you're a romance novel, cinematic in its conception
you laugh like butter, the sound knitting itself together in the dark

you put your hand on my stomach
        touch the edges of flesh, drag a finger across the crevice of the fupa
        it's a pagan prayer, singling out each insecure part of me to love

the shit movie is still playing on the old television & the catharcism is about to reach a climax

I open my mouth to kiss you & you shush me, the sound rising from your lungs
gutteral and distinct
        the sincerity, you whisper

SPRING

have you ever wondered why
ficases elope like that?
petals collapse onto hard wood broken
and bleached from years of openness
i am jealous of the ability they have
to be vulnerable in a concrete world
grey roads against crushed blossom
my heart is a cactus imprisoned all year
i let you touch its petals.

READ RECEIPTS ON

I want to consume you

jump into you and wear you like a Burberry coat

show you off—*this old thing? I found it in a charity shop for a quid!*

bask in you like a Brit abroad in Benidorm smothered in tanning oil SPF 4
        photographed in a Martin Parr exhibition

slurp you like strawberry milk, drink you in and keep drinking you

roll around in you like a pig in shit, one of the fat ones who'd make really good bacon

hang off every syllable you give me like a family playing charades at Christmas
        assess every movement as if it could be a clue to a cold case

lick you like the wooden spoon stirring grandma's chocolate cake recipe
        taste the salt on your skin left by sweat from walking weird September heat

pull you like the moon pulls the tides in

bathe in you like Cleopatra bathed in milk, a hundred handmaidens waiting to dress her

cover you in rose petals like that scene in the hunger games
        love can be just as violent as the Romans

Oh god, I'll talk to you like a Catholic grandma talks to Jesus, incessantly

I want to devour you like a roast dinner on a Sunday hungover as fuck
a bottomless brunch with Bloody Marys instead of mimosas

make you sweat like an old man in a sauna or a fuck boy in a group chat with two of
   his girlfriends

forgive my astrology chart drowning in water signs.
Read: emotional as fuck. Read: three
emotional breakdowns for breakfast,
text me back, please?

YOU'RE ON MY MIND

Golden Shovel for Tom Misch

                                            Whenever you listen to Tom Misch I
                        hope you think of me   I hope you can't
                    help but think of us side by side, heart stop-
  -ping   as you playfully carry me into July waves   I am thinking
                 about the shape of your lips as I cling to the outside of
              your knee   Dry grass in summertime brings images of you
      sat in the direct eyeline of the sun cradled in its glory   like
     a god at the top of a tall mountain I won't climb   I let the
         pebbles cling to my back, forcing indents into my spine for five
              whole minutes   Blood aches, muscles pound
                  & my brain sings *let go* but I won't   Not when you
look at me like that, not when 'The Journey' comes on shuffle and I demand you owe
me a kiss halfway down the motorway   who takes the wheel?

TODAY THE SKY IS A SCRATCHCARD

and i'm not even on acid but i swear there is molten honey behind the grey like

René painted half the sky and covered the rest with a game out of boredom

lick me out and produce a penny from my lips to scratch it with

reveal the prize like a rain shower after a long drought

and when i'm lying in your bedsheets after dark draw blood

enough for me to tell you 'i don't know why i'm bleeding'

substitute my jackpot for the sea that meets the skyline

thrive with me in this inflatable moment, push hard enough to make it burst

we both know nothing we make between our bodies

could ever be as permanent as the waves

that continue to batter the shoreline.

SUMMER

Sandpaper kisses gently erase dead skin past love
left coarse. The edges of your lips are still cracked.

I run my finger over them hoping to translate. You
won't speak about the past. I don't dare open up

the future. Each line on your face when you frown
at your phone tells me a story I learn nothing from.

I see the way you peruse. Pucker up, vampire
I'll let you take everything from me. This is only

the beginning. The red hot poker of passion. I look
again at your lips, dripping with the start of

something. How many times has love dripped
from them. How many times have they been

false promises. We are all guilty. We all live
in fear of our own actions. I reach for

your hand and instinctively you look at me. Remind
myself love is not an only child. It takes a village. It

takes a fucking stadium to kick a ball against a brick wall.
Maybe this time we won't die inside. It is 9pm and the

sun is still making shapes on the walls of the room.
Love can kick the life out of you at any time.

ELLIPSES

You are afraid to send me songs incase I read too much into the lyrics.
What am I supposed to do? I live between the space between words
their inflections   a party in the speed of sound.
A long walk into the ocean the sadness of it
ellipses in its simplest form - the language in which it was birthed
as in silence.   I am obsessed when you use it
dot dot dot a gavel on the corner stone.
What did you want to say   when you didn't?
Why are words never enough to describe this?
I think about sending you The Glass Essay by Anne Carson
but I don't.   I'm afraid you won't read into it enough

CHARLOTTE SAYS NO MORE LOVE POEMS

For Charlotte Shevchenko Knight

only regret
suck me through a plastic straw, spit me out
on wood i cannot bear to lie in another boy

only death
but what is grief if not love screaming in the shadow of a ghost?
what is a love poem if not wrapped in lust, the chaos of it

revenge, hate
your finger dancing along someone else's habit
the proof of it, another four-letter word
for the way we wrap our lives around expectation

Charlotte says no more love poems
only life

but what is life if not an arduously-long-sometimes-complicated love poem?
write me a eulogy leave all the details of my voice
to a history textbook, never fully tangible and

I don't want to mourn the way holding hands with your lover on a cold morning
or placing a Fanta Fruit Twist on their kitchen counter after a rough night
are love poems
written in the silence of a sleepy morning
watching a chest dance with sleep

what is love if not writing language like a puzzle
for that person to read it and say woah
I didn't know you could love me this much

I READ YOUR MESSAGES AGAIN

hoping to find a secret in the pixels   a love letter is not a love letter
unless there's paper   download me into an early grave
my brain is sick from the cold intimacy of seeing you're online
when you kiss me you call yourself a bastard   am i the antichrist?
the devolution of the catholic institution of marriage?
over 500 days of this the dopamine is wearing off   dread has moved
into my stomach making me eat the uncertainty   i can only decode
so many times   it's hard to wake this morning from dreams of you
and this poem is not a poem it's a warning   a work of fiction
that holds itself in no esteem   a poem cannot be a text asking you to call me
do you know how many ways there are to describe the colour blue?
over fifty seven shades of navy, royal, cobalt, indigo, cerulean
imagine an infinity more to describe sadness, loneliness, enlightenment
i read your messages again   call myself the ocean, all teal and buoyancy

think about touching you.

POEM IN RESPONSE TO YOUR PHONE CALL AFTER VALENTINE'S DAY

When you wake up, head ablaze with a thousand forgotten memories and your skin soaked through with dead sweat

I will not arrive on a white horse   clawing tesco bags filled with everything edible and beige insert lacklustre arms as a blanket around your body   wipe the smell of yeast from your brow.

I refuse.

Seeing as I do not arrive to soothe you, I will not be a body adding to the foundation of a house you have built to rot

I will not be there to soak up the lies that pour out of you.
     I will be asleep in my own bed dreaming new ways to develop a plot twist and forgetting you were ever a part of my plans.

A SHORT HISTORY OF THE BEDS WE HAVE SLEPT IN TOGETHER.
After Kei Miller

the 1s we never left all day   1s we wrapped up in when the world was spitting ice into the vent
       1 duvet / make it 2 the chill in the air crept past the flesh and into the major organs
remember when all we needed was the promise of a late night to keep us warm
       4 makeshift bed in tents   half-deflated from the weight of baggage   too heavy
to talk about   too much to discuss this far down the line   *didn't we bring
enough air for 1 lifeboat?*   I guess we'll float somehow   beds below sea level in february
heat   sweat patch stains   countryside murder cottages   how many
arguments has a hotel bed seen?   how many more?   1 barn in the country side to house
 a small army   1 knife left on the side waiting for us   call your mother   tell her you love her
      call your girlfriend   the other ones   x how many? 2? 3?
darling you did not need the knife to stab me   having already carved away my self respect
      I died in your bed reading a letter from someone else who once slept in it

SAVIOR COMPLEX

A golden shovel after Phoebe Bridgers' Savior Complex

i only started calling you baby
after i read it in a romance novel. you're
a peach to pretend you like it. a
real hollywood talent. a cowboy. a vampire.
a man misunderstood. you
have a history i will never unearth but damn, i want
to suffocate in your blood.
we go for a drive in the dark and
you let me sit in the passenger seat, i
don't ask if you've been drinking. i promised.
i like to think i'd be a good mob wife. which is a lie. i'm
too squeamish. when you watch a
gangster film i turn my eyelids inside out, *he's the bad*
guy, you are exacerbated by my performance. liar.
no less violent to murder someone with
a pillow. i hide beneath your forehead, your eyes a
patio awning to my thoughts. let you act the savior
for once. both know this is my complex.
less god, more mother theresa, more all
women who've ever thought of changing him. the
movie ends, i no longer see you as the hero. your skeletons
are too blatant for me to ignore the truth now. you
don't love me. still, i dig deeper into your arms. hide
further in the blood. already dead, nothing to show
for it. the gravestone you picked for me
reads: she was loved. the love was not yours.
calculate your remorse. error 404. i watch the film alone and
imagine you as the actor. this time, ill
and shaking with sickness of evening, i watch the gun show
in slow motion. imagine they are murdering you.

WHEN WE BROKE UP

It takes a whole year for the yolk
to drip all the way down your chin.

Yellow as a nursery rhyme, it whispers
ancient tragedies to me in comforting linguistics

as it crawls, hair by hair, engulfing each syllable
spat from your mouth in a dandelion blanket.

Dandelions have always fascinated me. Once I pointed
out to you how they start gold and new yellow,

then start to grey around the edges, become the mouthpiece
by which new children tell time. You agreed, how obviously

they seemed to age. How I would kill to be unburdened
by the passing of days, sun dials only a platform to worship

nature. My eyes leave the daydream and
turn to the river still forming on your face.

It looked so potently the start of something.

INFIDELITIES

burnt orange november light streams through windows
our island reminisces / oh how it feels to be summer

we sweat under two duvets one would be enough
clammy limbs fused together / Henry Moore

or maybe another less modern sculptor / less unsure
on what love might mean between two bodies

we have been through enough / I am scared to
shift the balance / melt your metal away

infidelities ghosts occupying my mind / an old creaky house
owned by a Disney witch, always the worst / never that bad

my brain is in the midst of battle / alert by creaks in the staircase
wondering who you have sent to kill me, my brain

a slideshow of dark rooms, you with other bodies moulded
together pulsing / I lie still eyes closed dreaming

wide awake / analysing the way Matt Damon in Good Will
Hunting draws on chalkboards / nothing left to lose

you are heroin I am Ewan McGregor in Train Spotting
the last time you shoot me up before we kill the baby

choose life, I guess. at least the possibility of change.

ON SOME SCORPIO SHIT

I offered myself to you on a platter made of gold, told you to place me next to you. Instead, you took a gold knife and carved my chest open. I didn't know I was bleeding until it was too late, saw my heart showcased on a plate (gold) and I watched you carve it (open). Piece by piece. You carved it. You carved it the way I imagine Clint Eastwood would eat an apple (you know, really cool). Knee up leaning back. Cowboy boots. Penknife tearing the skin from limb. Each cut tore the flesh, did you savour it? Or was it nothing but junk food to you? A drive-through. Beige. Replaced with golden arches, a paper bag stained with grease. Chucked in a bin. Hit and run. Left to sew myself up with the gold chains the necklace you bought me hangs from.

RUTH'S POEM

For Ruth Boon

I want to write a poem about heartbreak,
but I don't want to be soppy about it. I've spent
too many lines comparing you to the weather.
Instead, I'm going to write a poem how Ruth would.
She would look at this and say I knew it. She'd say love
feels like a tractor churning up wet mud on cold mornings
on the kind of farms where they turn new-born baby calves
to veal, which is to say, not very nice. She'd say something like
Love is like sitting backwards on a southern train that's been
diverted through Littlehampton, sometimes it makes you nauseous.
She'd be specific about it. I know what she'd say about this.
She'd say I told you so, but she'd say it in a disjointed and
poetic kind of way and also say that he's a dick and a man
playing with your heart like a child under the age of five plays
with an old baby born, which is to say not very carefully,
is not worth good dick. She'd tell me to stop being so romantic
about it, stop using rose petals falling and birds chirping to translate
a feeling which is really just a chemical reaction, not too dissimilar
to the one I feel when I smoke tobacco rolled in non-branded Rizla paper.
Ruth smokes tobacco between her middle and ring finger, like the only
entity she could see herself committing to is a cigarette.
Ruth would be happy I'm getting over you. She wouldn't tell me
to write your name on a piece of paper and burn it, she doesn't believe
in witchy shit. She'd tell me to imagine you as the piece of paper instead
scrunch it up and throw it against a brick wall painted off-white,
the kind of colour kids bounce half deflated footballs against at school.
I imagine you are the half-deflated football, and I am Beckham's right foot,
just the right one, and I kick you against the wall until all the nitrogen
mixed with oxygen is gone and I've suffocated it to death.

I SAW A TWEET THAT SAID 'MEN BE LIKE "I KNOW A PLACE" THEN TAKE YOU TO THE LOWEST POINT IN YOUR LIFE'

and I wet myself laughing at the audacity it had to be so true.

Last night I dreamt of you with your new girl

and buried in its claustrophobic layers was the spike beneath my breast plate I get when I remember you have barely suffered for your sins.

She made awkward chat with me, your new girl, and told me of the baby boy you share together. I saw him then, glistening and golden in her arms, a cherub.

"It was a surprise to us all!" she said

and I told her I was happy for her with so much well-meant enthusiasm my teeth fell out. You, Joseph, father in name only, silently cursing in the background.

I don't believe in god but I prayed right there and then if hell existed it would burn up the wooden floorboards painted pink in her house and swallow you, right in the middle of a shit.

I'd be doing her a favour

her son would have less chance of learning narcissism through each of your limp words that fall out of your chest like blunt pins and needles.

If there was a god she would have killed us long ago for the sheer lack of respect we have for the planet, don't deny it

if she decided to instigate 'big flood pt 2', this time she wouldn't let us build an arc to shelter in, instead watch as a few of us clung to salvaged IKEA wardrobes

me, floating on a painted plywood dining room set and live tweeting my relief.

DREAMING OF MEN

      i.

When I dream I don't always know I'm dreaming, they're too real
It's like crossing a bridge in a Studio Ghibli film   breathe and I'm stuck there forever

I have a recurring dream where my feet won't work, turning in on themselves

collapsing in on each other like the colours in a kalidoscope and I can't walk
and whichever man I'm dreaming of that night (it's all men lately) has to be my crutch,
ferry me forward on our adventure.

Conjure myself a support system in the men I revere,   tell them hold me! comfort me!
in my reverie I bend them over drill four wheels into their feet

turn the muscles in their stomach to a dashboard
poke a nerve to propel us forward and carry me away from bad decisions.

I wonder if you have to leave every hospital in a wheelchair, or just the fake ones on TV?
How much does art really imitate reality?

Are we stuck in an earth-sized washing machine turning us round and round copying art
which copies us, which copies art which copies us

round and round bounce out of the steel drum clean and pristine with no marks, perfect
little versions of each other.

      ii.

The other day I dreamt you were dead. In a scene that felt very final and ultimate I put your lifeless body in the back of a moving van, the stereotypical New York sitcom heavy metal shutter ones. And I said goodbye as the van drove off into the dusty orange sunset. And I let dusty orange juice from the illusionary nectarine in my hand flow down my chin as I bit into it. Savouring the flavour. It felt more real than your love ever did.

SCORPIO SZN

After Supermodel by SZA and Doves by Phil Wilcox

The leaves are turning brown, there is an end occurring.
On the way to the tube station, I choke to death on a song
that is not peaceful, like drowning in a kelp forest
instead turns me into a ghost   a haunting within the platforms
of disused London tube stations
the air here more dank, vulnerable, hungry.
SZA sings to me about supermodels and fucking friends
you ever listen to a song so good it ruptures all the major organs at once?
       I've lost the ability to empathise
unless it can be rapped on a diss track or laid down on a bed of nails.
(in my death I still cry at the old texts you sent)
SZA tells her lover his dick held her hostage
so she couldn't leave and damn if I didn't throw up inhibitions
on the streets of Brixton
text you the same god damn thing.

The stars only align over the latter part of October
which is why SZA was on some Scorpio shit when she wrote Supermodel
why I block out memories of you cupping my ego with promises.

Throw me a nightmare instead, I'll lick the edges off it like a full dairy Magnum
       the kind to ruin a stomach
writhing in pain I'll allow it to seep into my bones
       still less dangerous than your words.

Outside the stations, children are pulling bed sheets over their heads in innocent abandon.
I hope they never understand what a ghost really is.

SOME MORNINGS I DON'T REMEMBER THAT I LOVE YOU

O peaceful feeling   tinged with sombreness
the way a lighter touches the hair on your knuckles
when you choke on a cigarette you don't smoke
some art is only palatable in the thick of it
poetry is only words when cold to it all
hardened like leftover ice on side streets
i examine the flesh around my heart for hard tips
lullaby them into a bath filled with chamomile and first kisses
tell them soften round the edges   they don't always listen
every body of water in the country is at least 20% polluted
the way every body of blood is at least 20% glass
i allow myself to drown in it   the blood
metal and stiff a womb ejecting what could have been
this morning i wake in it   sip tea instead of coffee
shower away the sweat of a bad dream   remember that i love you

PART TWO

*"I don't forgive you,
but please don't hold me to it"*

—PHOEBE BRIDGERS, 'KYOTO'

FOUND HOROSCOPE FOR A LEO RISING.

▮CONSIDER YOURSELF ▮▮▮▮▮▮▮▮▮▮▮▮▮AN
IDIOT.▮▮▮▮▮▮▮▮▮▮▮VAIN▮▮▮▮▮▮▮▮
CRITICISM. YOUR ARROGANCE ▮▮▮▮▮▮▮▮▮▮▮▮▮A▮
MOTHER ▮▮▮▮▮ SPEND ▮▮▮▮▮▮ TIME KISSING ▮▮▮

PARENT TRAP (1998)

Both Lindsay Lohans in The Parent Trap forgive their parents too easily.
They grew up for 11 years thinking they had one parent and no sisters
and all of a sudden they realise they are a whole twin! A twin
that they shared their first home with, for 9 months
a digitally enhanced version of themselves! How could you forgive her for it?
A mother leaving one of her children on the other side of the world?
I still haven't forgiven my mother for accidentally throwing out my Nike sports dress
that I was going to wear to the year 6 leavers disco. I still think about it
the black and pink height of fashion. This thought keeps me up at night,
stops the blood coming at regular intervals. I imagine The Parent Trap
remade as an indie film, desperate for emotional trauma it will start
with a face on interview - a talking head except they are at therapy
(because one person in that film should have suggested therapy)
and Lindsay Lohan is discussing her failure to commit to a healthy relationship,
asking a stunned therapist why.

AUTUMN

The days melt together. Somewhere
a mother is burning bones.

It is a message to her children
see what happens when we rebel?

All parents' advice haunts us in the end.
Nearly the season for it, bed sheets

and black nylon do not offer up the
past as freely as a mother, touching

her child's temple, pleading with
them to be safe.

I ASK MY MOTHER ABOUT LOVE

questioning whether she has the same definition for loyalty.

Yes

she says.

MEN MAKE ME THIN

It's as if I can survive on lust alone
The adrenaline a three course meal
stuff my face with the validation of
a cat call *You should stay like this*
my mother says I forgive her in theory
she was brought up this way
I eat bread again feel guilty for it
she doesn't know the pain my
heart took to get this chin

LEO (RISING)

I am pulling teeth from my mothers mouth
                                        easier than talking

blood pools in her cheeks the same way it does in mine

her teeth are sharp and cut holes in my chest cavity, I carry them in my heart

sometimes I think I am only half a person
half a daughter, half a child asking the moon to let me read one more chapter before she catches

sometimes I think I am only half entitled to the world
or a relationship that really means something
                                        the fire burns it down too quickly

it's easy to say you have a saviour complex, easy to bite the apple
                                      harder to live with the poison of it

my voice is hard when I speak to my mother, I cannot help it, I learnt from the best

we play fight with emotional manipulation to see who is tougher
                                      she is, she has never been to therapy

my years of it has made me soft, I'm not ready to give that up for the taste of victory

we sink into the story of an ITV drama, sparse dialogue and cool colour corrected screens

easier than talking.

RORY GILMORE DESERVED BETTER

Back at my parents' house for the third time
except I am nearly thirty and it is just my mum now.
The fact that I didn't grow up in these walls is the
walking stick I use not to trip over the gaping holes
in my life. Help me navigate the world again, mum
now that we are both alone and restless.
I didn't go to Yale but Rory was the one who inspired
me to fail in journalism, talk fast wit to my long
suffering parents. Now they are back
more wooden, less sepia, Rory is dealing with the way
life didn't turn out the way she wanted.
Same girl, same. I too thought I would be reporting
from the campaign trail, let the books I read
become my whole world. No, I do not think she is
the poster girl for success, nor does she deserve
the hate directed at her from Buzzfeed journalists
content with free food and office drinks on a Friday.
I saw myself in her at 16 and I see myself in her now
well lit with bad lighting, looking around her
childhood bedroom for signs of a well lived life.
In 'A Year in the Life' she clings to her project with
both hands, gets drunk and sleeps with a guy she
couldn't pick out of a line up. I wish
I could say I can't relate. Truthfully
I believe I could have written her.
Scared at the prospect of going into teaching
writing the book my mother always hoped
I would. Perhaps I am putting too much pressure
on Rory Gilmore as a figurehead in social commentary.
Perhaps I am still crying into my chopping board
once again blaming it on onions but alas.
If Rory Gilmore is nothing to the real world, at least
she is another character to take comfort in whilst
the flames envelop the walls.

WELL SOMEONE HAS TO BE RESPONSIBLE

After Anne Carson

When my blood boils to the surface and I cannot settle it with a wooden spoon
I hit myself over the head with an aptitude for healthy eating, tell my mother no,
I won't spoil my dinner, yes I'll have a glass of wine, yes, we did say we wouldn't
tonight. Blood is always described as thick but when it pours out of you, hot and
raging, it feels like a thread destined to break. My mother asks if I met any nice
men and I hold my tongue between my teeth like a man holding a fish on a dating
app. With purpose, with great pain. She knows this. We are both givers, too much
has been taken away. After I cook, she stands at the kitchen sink. Pondering.

MY FATHER WAS A CROW

just for one second
before the inevitable
phone calls   and news
and *how are yous*
littered airways

deep dark
foreboding

my father was a crow
dying to get in
mess   up
my   kitchen
and do other dad crow like duties
clinging to the windowsill like a portal

think the newly painted ledge an alleyway
for caws to be sent to the dead

for just
one second

my father was a crow.

MIRROR, MIRROR

every time I get scared to call the bank I think of
the pink shoes you bought me in the market
how happy you could make a child for 2 euros
and I know you wouldn't have paid in euros because
they didn't exist till 1999 but I can't be bothered
to convert the price into pesetas at least not for this poem
because this poem isn't about politics but parenting
and how scared I am to grow anything incase I look
into the mirror and see it crumbling into debt
a money plant climbing the walls for an inch
of sunlight I forgot to give

I STOP DRINKING FOR A MONTH

to spite the way i look like my father
pour early morning sunrises down my throat
can i wake up to the birds for once
i wonder what they are discussing
a district council caw meeting
zoning ordinances and parking tickets
i feel guilty they don't know i am listening
my heart sitting silent on my tongue
still i fall asleep again
if my eyes grew legs they'd collapse
twenty seven years of this
and i am as solid as a butter knife
which is a lie, i am, in fact, the butter
forever going soft under pressure

I ASK MY FATHER ABOUT LOVE

questioning whether he has the same definition for regret.

No

he says.

I MEET YOU AT THE MILE STORE

you give me an inch and tell me to get going
it's not going to run on its own

after circling the aisles looking for an exchange rate
i take it to the counter, they don't accept it
it's legal tender

i turn to look at you but you are already gone, besides
you were only jars of honey stacked in a trench coat

i am talking to someone new
every time they don't text me back i want to take an old biro
one that doesn't work anymore, nib covered in dirt, dry ink and desperation

stab it in my leg missing all my major arteries dying slowly and painfully
from infection

except i don't actually want to do that
not really

the teenager behind the counter asks if i really want to buy the mile

because contrary to popular belief a mile is still a mile
and also it's non refundable

i walk out empty handed

MY SISTER AND I DISCUSS YOU BEING NICE TO THE NURSES

agree it is a good sign

shouting is synonymous with pain

as is my silence

I pick up the phone, forget how to dial

wonder about the science of phone calls

if I've already turned my brain to mush

I am exploring west london for the first time

the kyoto garden is cold but full of people

I watch the koi fish appear from murky green

it is so beautiful I want to call you

explain the colour of the water

send you the song it reminds me of

I text my sister instead.

WHAT IS A TRUTH ANYWAY

the people beside me say my truth in earnest
conversation   i am drilling rusty screws into
my brain to lobotomise every time i described
myself as spiritual   i bet they are the kind
of people who get taken advantage of
by psychics   describe themselves as
grounded but when their pizza took too long to arrive
complained   asked for free nourishment
on a gluten free base   i would make a bet
with a fake italian loan shark in new jersey they
have never worked in hospitality   and
i don't count allowing fake fuckboys with long hair
access to their bodies   label it free
what do you think about being an aqua-rus?
spell without the eye   harder to see the bullshit
scorpios get a bad rep   but i've never met a serial
killer who was one   i visit terry blair, dean carter,
andrew cunanan and henry lee lucas   ask if they
met my ex at the last meeting   virgos who
kill   and who they are planning next
the people are still popping balloons up their arseholes
using nurturing in a sentence   i am reaching for
the gun on the table to shoot the last of my brain cells
except it is not a gun it is a phone   the bullet a text

I WISH I HAD BEEN NICER TO HIM BEFORE HE GOT CRAZY

After Anne Carson

It takes an hour for the nurses to let me into the ward
and even so I am not recognisably myself
all paper and plastic, my arms are scarecrows
warm and stiff, they have not made contact with my dad in years
here they hang limp around his neck as they ignore
the way a personality deteriorates with drink
Anne Carson writes about carrying clarity into the hospital
how it disappears from the task in front
so clinical and yet sticky with emotion
the tears have stopped but my face still resembles a rockpool
when I was a kid he used to play guitar with his left hand
crank Neil Young and Jimi Hendrix in the car
tell me bad words, beg me not to repeat them
when I finally step into the ward
filled with other men all equally deranged
I don't recognise him
his face is a language I have forgotten
all new slang and idioms in a foreign tongue
it's only when he swears, angry with the constraint of
addiction I hear him as a kid again, scared, alone

THE DRY HEART (1947)

A woman's heart was wet with salt, metal
and the memory of a dead child

Her husband's was sand and dust
and unfamiliarity

I knew a dry heart once too
it would suck the life out of a cockroach

I soaked a bandage in Irish whiskey
Lit it on fire, straight to the heart (my heart)
It gave me purpose, dried me out

The woman shot her husband
Between the eyes,
I drew a cross on my forehead.

FORGIVEN LOVE

      Soft
each touch to your cheek after a tear has parted seas among hairs, *soft*
as in every new leaf that leaves a secular piece of earth   beautifully maintained in reinforced
circular plastic   *soft*   is the smell of tea tree oil in hot water   *you feel soft*
    like patiently emerging from said water   enraptured in a cloak of cooling edges
      retreating into curvatures under your wayward thumb my lips part for *soft* sentences to
ooze from them   each one a drip of honey   ambrosia   amnesia
    memories belong in hard water   instead give me your hand   *soft*
      devoid of calluses   *soft*   satin bricks   steady in their need to hold my
 body   electric and needy   once again   *Soft.*

PART THREE

"And why do I want? I want to live and feel all the shades, tones and variations of mental and physical experience possible in my life. And I am horribly limited."

—SYLVIA PLATH

"We should meet in another life, we should meet in air, me and you."

—SYLVIA PLATH, 'LESBOS'

FOUND HOROSCOPE FOR A PISCES MOON

███████ A VIVID IMAGINATION ██████████████ YOU ARE ████████
████████████████████████████ INFLUENCE ███ YOUR FRIENDS █████
RESENT YOU ███ FLAUNT ███ YOUR POWER. ████████ CONFIDENCE AND
████████████████ DISASTER.

HOW TO WORSHIP

I am going to write a poem that is so moon
other poets will fall at my feet,
cover their cheekbones in cream cheese
for me to lay stale crackers on their noses.

My moon poem will be so evangelical
1000 samurais would rather fall on 1000 swords
every time the sun rises than spend one full day awake
unilluminated by the white eye of the universe.

I am going to write a poem that is so moon
everyone who believes in jesus will feel foolish
the only time they've seen their deity is by staring
at 1000s of drawings of a white man in sandals.

I am going to write a poem that is so unbelievably moon
those who live guarded by darkness and death
metal will eat their shoelaces when I tell them
the moon dies each month only to live again,

like the sun setting, flowers blooming and Jesus, christ
and crisp like the apple tree that grows to make
shit cider drunk on street corners by men who
can't bear to go home and cry themselves to sleep.

I am going to write a poem so moon, so fucking moon
that the big buildings made of stone and stained glass
directing light through blood red lose the power to make
knees weak enough to pray the darkness away.

Instead, my moon poem will convert skeptics
from the darkest corners of the internet
because her shape is supple as the letter
and her form could never be anything but hourglass.

My moon poem will reveal her face to be
the most ancient of clocks, replace sundials
with moon watches, each time she blinks we
fall deeper into shadows and closer to soft mud.

This poem will be so moon, every time the sun comes back
he will die with jealousy at her freedom fighters
eternal eclipse, us, silver concrete and limbs
closer to the earth and memory that if nature wants to kill she will.

JEALOUSY IS MY LOVE LANGUAGE

two sparks meet over a lit bonfire
a motorbike made of glitter and cutthroats
screams on its maiden voyage
this is the sound of a sacred heart
and by that i don't mean blessed by jesus
but doused in petrol and set on fire by the thought
that someone else may have something that i want
don't misunderstand
i would rather fuck you than fight you for it
jealousy is a secret language you can whisper in my ear
whiskey breath and dressed in black
i'll hate you so much i'll love you even more
tell me of your accomplishments
i'll roll my eyes as i simp for you
letting my knees fall to the tiled floor of the studio flat
which i would never do for anyone i felt remotely secure with
only after i've crucified myself with such devotion
home alone nursing my bruises back to pink
under mundane darkness a spark sets everything alight

WINTER

Memories flock like starlings. Pull out the sofa
bed, bring the birds to us. Lie back on the beach
stones, watch them dive dipping under each
burnt bone of the West Pier. I live forever in those
moments, flight before the fall. I don't mind the
heartbreak, too often we let the sadness of the ending
overshadow the art. I don't know if I remember
the same things I used to. If I were a starling
I wouldn't leave to come back for the winter.
Long after the season I would stay and create
patterns in the wind over the sea, begging you
watch as I death dive, each fall broken by waves.

THE WEST PIER IS STILL BURNING

a skeleton sits not too far from the coast
dark black, a home for birds after sunset
they ask why you haven't torn her down yet
a modern ruin, a noughties baby, a new look
for an old friend. can't you see? i ask tourists
clutching paper wrapped fat. the west pier is still burning.
look closely, see her wrapped in amber,
preserved in the memory of teen drinking
stomach pump. a badge connecting honour and
shame. concrete bowls. old graffiti tags. way before
the souvenir shops and overpriced seafood shipped
in from spain. a few years ago they retrieved
her guts from the sea bed. they light them up now
each night a jazz band with two drummers and
a name i never remember play between them, dirges
dressed in ¾ time. i remember the day she was
plastered all over newspapers. front pages hot for
three whole days. they say it was arson but could
never prove it. the evidence burnt away then washed
out after low tide. now she is pure carbon. a marker
to prove how we must ruin everything. there are
whispers of an eye sore, sure. it's only new blood
who ask you what they plan to do with it.
didn't you know? we say, the west pier is still burning
ash and dust coat our lungs so that we may choke
on the memory of her long after the last of her
bones wash away by the unrelenting sea.

ALL THE MEN ARE CRYING

because i have vowed to take them all down
from the inside - not in high heels but big black
boots and fila destroyers their groins blood and throat
squirming and screaming like a horror film actor
who deserves to die. my vengeance is a voodoo doll
pinned together by bobby pins left underneath
your pillow to ward off other women who i whisper
sweet nothings to, they are also women so they
understand what sweet nothings amount to
[evaporating clouds climbing away from the earth]
i envy the floating clouds their ability to float
i too would suffocate myself in the sky for the myth
of a man who loves. all the men are crying
not because of the descent of the planet into the gap
between fire and ice, but the consequences
of their own actions exacerbated by gratuitous nudity.
i make a dickpic masterpiece downloaded from the cloud
and let them deepthroat the shame when i show them
to their mothers. all the men are crying, and by all the men
i mean you, or you will be.

AT ETERNITY'S GATE

After Van Gogh

Outside looks like a Van Gogh painting
and I want to cut off my ear to better
understand how it can be so beautiful when
reflected through raindrops lingering on plastic
rimmed double glazed windows. If I were to cut
it off with a pair of blunt nail clippers, maybe I could
use the shooting blood from the severed artery in my
neck to create a masterpiece on white bed sheets
that screams 'no one understands me' in a stereotypical
struggling artist way. Maybe, one day, they will hang it in a
futuristic art gallery next to a Pollock. When I
finally bleed out from my badly butchered ear, I will
arrive in a small and unassuming but ultimately quite
quaint cafe that acts as a holding place for dead artists
who died in a very traditionally artistic way (seeing as they
can't affect the rest of the afterlife with melancholia).
I will see Van Gogh sitting quietly to himself. I will go up
to him and sit, speak to him in broken French about what
a treasure he turned out to be. He will look back with eyes
glazed over like motor oil on a puddle and an expression
that reads 'I don't understand your broken French' and
simultaneously 'your eyes do not convey an understanding
of the amount of pain that mine could possibly have gone
through.' After this I will sit, in this extraordinary kitsch cafe
with handmade tables and chairs, all with one leg slightly
infuriatingly shorter than the other, and awkwardly sip scotch -
my third favourite whiskey - without ice from a warm glass
and indulge my imagination in what it would have been like
to see the street lamp as it was; a Romanian invention that
ups the quality of modern life by about 20% instead of a
message in the madness to lead me here, a four walled
room that could be anywhere in Europe but isn't, daydreaming

of Earth, where I no longer am, full of thousands of
people equally wondering whether or not to leave it.

WE HAD A MOMENT TO REFLECT AND WE CHOSE NOT TO

For Dakota

We sit on the train the same way we always have and flinch at the sound of a cough.
A cough is just a cough until it kills you, the same way rain is just rain until it takes you away with it. Not close. Still, stiff. This is the way we have always been. We learn then forget.
Fickle & flimsy, a necklace from Claire's Accessories waiting to break. In the early hours of morning I research herd immunity. How do vaccines work a four day week? They lied to us about the Venice canal. There were never any dolphins. Fewer schoolchildren died of an asthma attack in 2020.
I wrap my fingers around a cup of tea, wonder what they did to grow it. I do not turn the heating on. The word virus has entered the membrane of our vocabulary and we can't stop saying it.
Spit it out onto a piece of tissue and examine it under the microscope. Is it looking in a mirror? Do we gawk like a budgie at our own irrelevance? How does something insignificant destroy so much? I ask the same of my brain before each sleep. We've only been to the moon once, I like to think she put a curse on us. How dare we disturb her nightly race against the day. All the good the space did us has evaporated. Dignity is just a word unwriting itself into each day.
We had a moment to reflect and we chose not to. Yes, but there's always next time.

IF WHAT RUMI SAYS

After Rumi

that we began as mineral is true
infuse my whole life with the flavour of it
if i bathe in a pool glistening with the light
of the moon on the cusp of the spring and the
solstice promise me that i'll never forget the way we emerged
from dirt and dust and deteriorated from
organic matter of the universe
artichokes are not the only ones with hearts covered in a cage
and they are not the only ones with hearts at all
sometimes i think we forget how there is a centre of us
just as there is with the cabbage, the apple core, the olive stone,
the artichoke the snail the ex lover the earth,
the dandelion, as it starts to unfurl again in spring
ageing before our eyes, gold, grey and gone.

CAREFUL OUT THERE THE WORLD IS BURNING

i am etching a spell into your palm with
a thousand kisses on the same spot
worry is a currency that cannot buy anything
if i were to cut open a circle beneath your feet
allow us to fall all the way through
how deep could we go before we noticed we were already burnt
flesh and bone, stubborn as behaviour
soft as the unbearable lightness of life
how confronted with the earth's core would we have to get
to realise the world has always been burning
permanently regurgitating heat
i can feel it when i succumb to anger and bang
my fists against the side of your mother's touch
gripping onto the blood in your heart, i pray for stability
we watch netflix in bed
let crumbs make a map on dirty sheets
here we don't think about the future
there is no soap that can remove
the headlines from the back of my eyelids
and the night has never felt so calm now
i know it is the real constant of the universe
why worship the sun when it only proves
how scorched we all are
you leave to buy sparkling water
be careful out there the world is burning
but you don't hear me, you are already dead

THE WOMAN ALWAYS WEARS HER LOVERS SHIRT

the red blood of morning swims on my lovers eyelids as I
                                        reach out and glide my hand over each lash

        they sway under my fingertips

they dance the nutcracker under each groove

                I raise my lips to their cheek, no kiss

a caress, a little reassurance to make it through the night,
        an archway when the morning hasn't completely broken down into day

my lover sleeps and I tell them stories through weighted palms

praying in the gaps between their spine
        and when they stir, I tiptoe out of bed in an oversized cotton shirt

and put the coffee on whilst parents take their kids to school in the world outside my window

this is sex depicted in movies with new york sunlight streaming in from LA sets

the woman always wears her lover's shirt

she swims in waves of cotton, wrapped in sheets and chalk and sea salt
                                        she is a duvet and the shirt is a duvet cover
                engulfing her

I do not wear my lovers shirt

the lovers grazing my bedsheets adorn wardrobe choices I am unable to sail

sawn off sleeves from band shirts I've never heard of will not preserve my dignity as the water
                                                                                                                         in the kettle boils.

      my lovers do not wear shirts that billow in the summer evening breeze

I bought my own

          tucked under pillowcases for late night phone light excursions

blue pinstripe rivers gently push me upstream

                          as my lover snores soundly

CONSCRIPTION

i imagine the letter will be heavy
that it will fall through the metal
like a heart ripped from a chest
saturated with blood and the promise of it
land on the doormat ready
to drag you through mud
sometimes i pace the fake wood
waiting for it to come, i
sing to the birds, ask them
to form a choir to raise morale
wonder if they mind me writing about them
sometimes the letter is light as feathers
as if it could float away at
a moments notice because what is life
if not the heaviest and lightest of things
the trivial come alive by fire
sometimes the letter comes to me
in dreams thick with ink and words
ancient letters arriving at understanding
because what else is there
to be pushed into a fight we can never win
sometimes, buried in my own thoughts
i wish for the letter
something to actively object to
i am getting tired of waiting for a riot

THE SEA WILL KILL YOU IF SHE WANTS TO

Ekphrastic poem after Alexandra Kehayoglou's tapestry.

Years too long ago to count, a grandmother told her grandaughter
I hope your voyage is a long one. These words are best remembered
driving through the island of Lesbos in the winter, where you'd be forgiven
for thinking you were closer to the Celts than the Med. The grass a vibrant green,
rocks penetrating each cusp. Yes, these are olive trees but suspend your eyes
for a moment. Imagine only emeralds. You only see the work nature poured into this place
when you have time you don't want. We wish our voyages quick and painless.
Children ask are we there yet out of habit. I was one of them. We want to be out of the rain
instead of stuck in it. *There is a mountain of salt in a riverbed somewhere near here.*
So we drive to it, see the flamingos noticeably white. Wonder about their sodium intake.
Once there was an exhibition with dancers on top of the salt. Once these tapestries
were displayed in a shop window to sell luxury items to companies that make money
cutting down the rainforest in the artist's home country. Once a month a body washes up on the
shore here. *Three this year.* Pushed back from safety, a short voyage. Three is a big number
in death. It's a delicate balance, being a citizen of the world. The grandmother says
you cannot have both. She makes the rugs by hand. I wonder how many fingers it would take to
unravel, the green forming tufts around my nails as they turn red and white from
pressure. I twist until it looks like mould on my skin. Funny. Maybe we are nothing.
Maybe we are the problem. I don't know when we will destroy the planet
but I don't think it will take long. Perhaps this is why the grandmother wishes us time.
Tells us to walk the long way home. Perhaps this is why we cannot see the woods
through the trees. It is all one picture. When I say goodbye to my loved ones
I whisper *I hope your voyage is a long one.* But at the end, once the hills and the sea
and the miles of green thread used in these tapestries has turned toxic to touch,
dear god, I hope our deaths will be quick.

RING

sometimes i put a cheap ring on my finger and pretend somebody loves me

sometimes i put a diamond ring on my finger and pretend somebody loves me

the effect is the same

a ring is just a ring until somebody loves you

and whilst there's nothing particularly wrong with that

it doesnt mean anyone loves me

last night i woke up drenched in the fear that one day i will have to open up to someone new

wrap my insecurities in coca cola and chase them down with a childhood memory

a funny one that takes the trauma away and

every time a man calls me beautiful i wonder how many other women he's fucking

because isn't that what men do when they want to keep you contained

and fuck i forgot to take the ring off

everyone in the queue for train tickets out of blackfriars station thinks somebody loves me

for a moment i let myself believe it

MOON POEM

After Moon Song by Phoebe Bridgers

i would so desperately like for you
to leave me in the morning with
no more than a dirty tissue

i want your bad breath to linger on mine
the whole sulphuric morning
because then at least i have some proof

that way i won't have to continuously
look at the moon wonder how to lasso it
my brain always searching for the right words

to convince you to give me the sky
instead of remembering the feel of your chin
against mine as we told each other we shouldn't do this

I ASK MY SISTER ABOUT LOVE

questioning whether she has the same definition for heartbreak.

No

she says.

I tell her she's wise,

Thanks

she says.

I learnt everything from you.

SIBLING RIVALRY

My sister is a baby pink letter, her kindness a knife. I am gum, chewed up and spat out. Gold in the morning, dark purple at night. My kindness is a fork, pointed. We walk like lemons rolling down hills. Our bond is a spoon, full and feeding.

A MOST SATISFACTORY DREAMLIFE

After Anne Carson

I am listening to the wind bang its fists on the window dreaming of a way to make you real again

I have this power you see, to resurrect within my skull.

Sometimes my dreams are too real to pull from. More times than I care to admit I have woken up crying white streaks of salt forming paths on my skin.

Make the trip to the bathroom. Consider calling you, decide against it.

When I close my eyes I can create rows and rows of beaches where we repeat the same old shit. You meet me here and we walk into the sunset. An apocalypse where we are winning. A child you never knew existed.

In my dreams I always find a new way to make you love me.

Someone once told me you either have a naked neighbour or you are the naked neighbour.

I never dare to close my blinds, it's hard enough to wake me as it is.

Not even the sun can tempt me to exist in the real world, where my brain operates at half capacity and your messages sit still in the archive section of WhatsApp.

And the thing is, I remember it all. All the words I've ever made you say to me, every touch from a childhood crush, every mean-spirited thing or message never sent

so when I wonder whether I should have a man, get on with life

I think about Emily Bronte, walking the moor, dreaming herself to death.

I AM WRITING YOU A LOVE POEM ALTHOUGH I KNOW YOU WILL NEVER READ IT

in the dark aftermath of love being lost
and the hope of it being recovered a bookie's
best dinner, i write you a love poem
the morning cold and hopeless
yet i still hear birds singing
gossip how many times you kissed me
before the sun came up
not that you ever got to see it
i want to tell you i remember the shape of your belly
your flesh pronounced in its proximity to mine
you leaned over and i saw all the colours in your hair
a painting i have not read the artist's interpretation on
i see blue and yellow and goddamn if you dare correct me
this is my poem
and in this poem i am telling you i love you
without malice / vested interest, alone in my bed
as the sky turns a neon peach without you to witness
and i am writing you a love poem
even though i know you will never get to read it

SEND MORE LIFE

After bot obituary and Frank O'Hara

Whilst you sleep I think of all the things I'd like to say to you,
but as soon as you wake, half-drunk with the potency of dreams,
I allow myself to forget. What are questions when you are right there
in front of me, golden with the edges of morning? I was thinking
of asking you to come to New York with me, just to see The Polish Rider
because it's in the Frick and although I do understand the draw
of looking at you rather than any other thing in the world,
I would still like to have you in New York, looking at a painting
so beautiful it inspired a love poem. I tell you about another poem,
actually an obituary written by a bot, but I tell you it's a poem
because right at the end, just when you are ready to forget it
along with 90% of things you read on the internet,
the nonsense that technology has made of us and this thing
we named language: in lieu of flowers, send Brenda more life.
As if this is achievable. Fuck the flowers, fuck the sympathies,
the thoughts and prayers. Send her back to us. I look at your back,
rising and falling as if bursting with forgotten potential.
Throw my phone against the wall, hope that it could stop the clock.
Never show me another sunflower, just send me more life.
Loving you in this one is not enough.

ONLY

In the dark I dare to imagine
which features our daughter will inherit
the bruising of her birth in my distant memory
the paradox of allowing her into a dying world.
I imagine her shouting blue murder into our faces
she never asked to be born.

At the park in Spring years from now
she points to a flower making its way through the grass.
Whats this? I tell her its a dandelion, the last of its kind
she goes to pick it and I stop her, tell her the bees will
come for it. *What are bees?* she asks, innocent as the season
realise she has never seen one. *Insects, buzz, make honey*
only exist in farms now. I watch her play with the grass,
yellow and twisted, again wonder if it was a good idea
to watch my belly grow with the expectation
of a healing wound. I tell her there used to be cups
of sunshine we put to chins to see if we liked butter.
What's butter? Something we used to eat.

STAY SOFT

I once saw feathers rain from the sky like a coronation of softness
I put my chin to it, wanted to catch the calm

Press it into my skull until I became patchwork

It was only later I learnt of the violence that would have had to occurred
collision of edges and flesh

I did not understand then how something so beautiful could be the end
a backbone breaking in the sky

My backbone bends a little more each time I fall

There is always violence in vulnerability
the edge of a hangnail as it parts a path on your stomach

I woke up that morning, bundled by a duvet alone
remembered all the words i said to you in the secret hours of the morning
cried for an hour

Allowed it to build and break like a wave, sighed
fortified myself with the sharp edges of a flume

It was only after I danced in the soft rain, screaming with joy for this gift
that my father took me gently aside, told me about the certainty of death

I cried for a week.

SPRING AGAIN

Sometimes I have these small pockets of calm
Like finding a curled up note in the pocket of blue denim
Or seeing a sunrise for the first time in six months
Where light hits my face, shining as a fresh pint in an old pub
Turns my cheeks gold with pregnant potential
And I realise I love myself just a little bit more than I did yesterday.

FRANK O HARA NEVER TWEETED

After 'Ode To Joy' by Frank O'Hara

we shall have everything we want and there will be no more dying

but let's pretend he did

that he was never struck down by a reckless driver drunk on youth

that he lived to kiss the thighs of a thousand more men

wrote a thousand more love poems referencing other popular beverages

whenever i see my father i pretend i am not related by blood

and it helps me believe i do not have a problem with my temper

until i can't help but vomit hot outrage at his feet, broken and hurting

like my heart after all the years i've spent working it to death

may the guilt remind us to do better next time

let's pretend that we are still friends, that birthdays will never again

end in tears, missed opportunities and stale cake

that sarah got home safely, that george is still breathing

that a boy walks into a shop and walks out again.

frank wrote no more dying but i am saying it now

to whoever can hear me, to lost cities

to each singular piece of the sky as it falls down my window i am yelling it into my pillow until my voice cracks

shards of hope like calls into plastic cups and

i hope that we are all secretly listening to each other

a network of feathers and damp cotton

even if the world won't.

NOTES

P. 5 - relates to this article by SZA https://www.cosmopolitan.com/entertainment/music/a10289867/sza-interview-ctrl/

P. 6, 29, 48 - found horoscopes all from excerpt from *Mother Jones Magazine*, Reddit article: https://www.reddit.com/r/funny/comments/r2qvk4/so_this_is_a_horoscope_originally_published_by/

P. 7 - 'Heartbreaker' - an earlier version of this was first published in *Ink, Sweat and Tears*.

P. 10 - 'Read Receipts On' - an earlier version of this appeared in *Dreich Magazine*.

P. 11 - Song reference is 'You're On My Mind' by Tom Misch, album Geography (2018).

P. 12 - René is a reference to René Magritte.

P. 18 - Title is in reference to a sequence with the same name by Kei Miller.

P. 19 - Poem is a golden shovel for the song Savior Complex found on Phoebe Bridgers album Punisher (2020)

P. 21 - Films referenced Good Will Hunting (1997) W. Matt Damon, Ben Affleck D. Gus Van Sant and Trainspotting (1996) W. Irvine Welsh, John Hodge D. Danny Boyle.

P. 23 - Ruth's Poem was first published in 'Anthology For A Friend' by *Lucent Dreaming Magazine*.

P. 26 - Poem references the song Supermodel by SZA off her album Ctrl (2017). The line 'that is not peaceful, like drowning in a kelp forest' is a reference to Phil Wilcox's poem 'Doves' which can be found in his collection Beetle Prayer.

P. 28 - Kyoto by Phoebe Bridgers, album: Punisher (2020)

P. 30 - Poem in reference to the film The Parent Trap (1998) W. David Swift, Nancy Meyers D. Nancy Meyers.

P. 35 - Poem's Rory Gilmore is in reference to character in Gilmore Girls created by Amy

Sherman-Palladino and portrayed by Alexis Bledel.

p. 36 - Poem's title is in reference to a line from Anne Carson's poem The Glass Essay.

P. 44 - Poem's title is in reference to a line from Anne Carson's poem The Glass Essay.

P. 45 - Poem is in reference to the novel The Dry Heart by Natalia Ginzburg (1947)

P. 46 - Forgiven Love was first published in *Hecate Magazine* (since defunct).

P. 47 - First Sylvia Plath quote is from *The Unabridged Journals of Sylvia Plath*, second quote from her poem Lesbos.

P. 49 - A poem in response to a niche poetry meme of Jane Lynch's character in glee saying 'I am going to create an environment which is so toxic' but instead it says 'I am going to write a poem which is so moon'. This poem was first published in *Porridge Magazine* online.

P. 55 - At Eternity's Gate references a painting by Sorrowing Old Man (At Eternity's Gate) made in 1890

P. 57 - Poem references excerpt from Rumi's "The Dream That Must Be Interpreted".

P. 59 - This poem was written in conjunction with the WRIOT collective workshops and an earlier version published in their zine.

P. 62 - Poem is in response to a tapestry collection 'Hope The Voyage Is A Long One' (2016) by Alexandra Kehayoglou - https://alexandrakehayoglou.com/Hope-the-voyage-is-a-long-one

P. 64 - Poem references Moon Song by Phoebe Bridgers off album Punisher (2020).

P. 67 - Poem's title is in reference to a line from Anne Carson's poem 'The Glass Essay' and also references themes from it.

P. 69 - The poem's title and themes is in response to 'Bot Obituary' (https://i.redd.it/pazmatx-5zvm71.jpg) it also references lines from Frank O'Hara's 'Having A Coke With You.'

P. 73 - Poem references poem 'Ode To Joy' by Frank O'Hara, as well as the Frank O'Hara bot on twitter. It also references a line from a poem by Roy McFarlane 'Rashan Charles, 2017' which references the death of a young black man by police. The Sarah in the poem references Sarah Everard who was murdered by an off duty police officer in 2021.

ACKNOWLEDGMENTS

This book has been a long time in the making, and there are a lot of people to thank.

Thank you first of all to Fern Angel Beattie. Angel is so fitting to be your middle name because this book, especially this version of it, would not exist without your support, your belief and your incredible drive. Thank you for seeing what you see in me, I hope I prove worthy of it.

Thank you Ollie O'Neill, my frequent collaborator and someone who I look up to regularly. Thank you also for introducing me to Fern.

Thank you Casey Ramar for being a beacon of wisdom and designing a beautiful book cover (again).

Thank you Scarlett Ward, you were the first person to edit this collection before it became this collection and I am so thankful for your continued support and friendship.

Ruth Boon, Charlotte Shevchenko Knight, Daphne Smith, Dakota Blue Richards thank you for reading this book in its earlier stages and giving me your honest opinions.

Thank you also to my WRIOT crew (past and present) for being the support system I always hoped for. Thank you to the other poets that inspire me on a daily basis, including but not limited to KT O'Pray, Cecilia Knapp, Connor Byrne, PJ, Roy McFarlane, Phil Wilcox and everyone who has ever attended Words By The Water.

Thank you to Dannie, Eleni, Ellie, Kit and all my beautiful friends who have helped me write this along the way. Thank you also to the friends I made in Greece and the island of Lesvos where I managed to finish this book.

Thank you to my family. To my mother and my father, for supporting me and believing in me even through all the storms. I wouldn't change a thing. To my little sister Meg, you are still my favourite person in the world.

Lastly, thank you to the people I fell in love with who inspired a lot of this poetry.

To everyone, stay soft.

ELLA SADIE GUTHRIE IS A WRITER WHO OFTEN FAILS AT BEING FUNNY. After studying her NCTJ and giving up on news journalism she moved into poetry. She has featured at an array of London poetry nights including Verses and Off The Chest and has performed at the House of Commons. She is the co-host of Words By The Water in Brighton. In 2019 she co-founded WRIOT, a poetry collective for women and non-binary poets. Her words have appeared in *Lucent Dreaming, Ink, Sweat and Tears, Hecate Magazine, Drawn to the Light* and *Dreich Magazine*. Her first pamphlet *Poems For Pete Davidson*, which explores the themes of fantasy, pop culture and ADHD was published by Broken Sleep Books in 2022. Mostly she spends her time walking along Brighton seafront and daydreaming.

If you like Ella Sadie Guthrie, Ella Sadie Guthrie likes...

What We Are Given
OLLIE O'NEIL

The Cardboard Sublime
OLIVER SEDANO-JONES

Look How Alive
LAUREN HOLLINGSWORTH-SMITH

Bloody beautiful books.

Write Bloody UK is an independent poetry publisher passionate about bringing the voices of UK poets to the masses. Trailing after Write Bloody Publishing (US) and Write Bloody North (Canada), we are committed to handling the creation, distribution and marketing of our authors; binding their words in beautiful, velvety-to-the-touch books and touring loudly with them through UK cities.

Support independent authors, artists and presses.

Want to know more about Write Bloody UK books, authors, and events?
Join our mailing list at:

WWW.WRITEBLOODYUK.CO.UK

More Write Bloody UK Books

What We are Given — Ollie O' Neill

Ping! — Iain Whiteley

Hard Summer — Francisca Matos

Small Machine — Demi Anter

The Cardbord Sublime — Oliver Sedano-Jones

Look How Alive — Lauren Hollingsworth-Smith

www.ingramcontent.com/pod-product-compliance
Lightning Source LLC
Chambersburg PA
CBHW020212090426
42734CB00008B/1037